Dip My Pacifier in Whiskey

Dip My Pacifier in Whiskey

Mathias Nelson

NYQ Books™

The New York Quarterly Foundation, Inc.
New York, New York

NYQ Books™ is an imprint of The New York Quarterly Foundation, Inc.

The New York Quarterly Foundation, Inc.
P. O. Box 2015
Old Chelsea Station
New York, NY 10113

www.nyqbooks.org

First Edition

Set in New Baskerville

Layout and Design by Raymond P. Hammond
Cover Illustration by ©istockphoto.com/Diana Walters

Library of Congress Control Number: 2011932517

ISBN: 978-1-935520-48-1

Dip My Pacifier in Whiskey

Acknowledgments

RATTLE, Gutter Eloquence, Cherry Bleeds, New York Quarterly, Nerve Cowboy, Epic Rites Press, Chiron Review, Poetry Warrior, Adagio Verse Quarterly, Exuberant Ashtray, Zygote In My Coffee, Suisun Valley Review, Underground Voices, Beat the Dust, Juice Press, Madswirl

Josh Olsen for introducing me to poetry and not being a dream-killer.

And thanks to William Packard, Raymond Hammond, and all others involved with the NYQ.

For those that find their loved ones disagreeable, but continue loving them anyway. And for the lost, the people without the answers—so pretty much everyone decent in this crazy humanity. This is for you.

Contents

Love Winter

Horripilation

Dip My Pacifier in Whiskey

I'm sober as the day I was born, and as terrified too.
Sometimes I think maybe I just need a spank
to let it all out. Preferably from a beautiful nurse
who doesn't care if I'm a young man with bald spots.
Even my dog looks at me with disgust.
I'm afraid to go outside and pick up his turds.
What if the neighbor asks me how I'm doing, or if I've found a job?
Oh God, you can't tell people you don't want to work. Why,
why do we have to ruin our knees and our backs,
deprive ourselves of sleep until we snap?
Oh God, it's freezing outside.
Steam comes out of my dog's butt.
He won't look at me anymore and
I think he has Obsessive Compulsive Disorder.
He has to sniff every turd before he comes in.
By the time he's done he's completely exhausted.
There's four-hundred eighty-two turds. I counted.
When will his tail wag? If I had a tail
it'd be wrapped around my little balls to keep them warm.
Last time I left the house I fed bread to the deer. Then the DNR called,
someone had complained, ratted me out for being nice.
I told the DNR I was feeding da birds, and he called me a liar,
threatened to take my money. Oh God, why do we need it?
Money. Without it they won't let me live on this land.
I don't want to live on this land, but where to?
I guess the Mississippi islands are my last chance,
but I'm afraid of the DNR. I just need a woman,
but women terrify me! How can something make babies?
What kind of voodoo magic is this? Oh God, old people wear diapers too.
Is that why we call it mother Earth, because we will be swallowed
by the Earth's pussy all over again? Oh Jesus, I hope I didn't offend
anyone by saying pussy...cunt, no! Vagina!
I don't want anyone to come after me, really, I'd like to live
in the middle of a mountain with a long, thin airway cut to the top.
That way a little light would get in, and rain too.
I don't need food. I swear I could live off my nails.

13

I think they're after me though, the people who saw me feeding the deer.
It's probably the park owners. Every winter they let the blind and disabled
hunt in the park. The deer come right up to the cars and BAM.
I've eaten all my toenails. Probably won't have food
for another week now. If only I had a cow,
the calcium would help. I'd suck it right out the udders,
pretend they're a mother's nipples. Not my mother's—
that's disgusting! I'm such a baby, hear my cries…
let me rest my head on your chest. Maybe all I need
is mounds of fat to cover my eyes and ears.
But what if I forget to take off my glasses
and they break. And what if the breasts
are made of silicone, and my broken glasses
pop them open. I won't be able to see.
Will there be a sudden breast wind?
Will I drown in some strange liquid?
What if I think it's milk and drink it?
Will it kill me? Killed by a mother's breasts?
See, nothing is safe. I'm terrified,
sober as the day I was born.
Please, spank me so I can breathe again
I assure you it is not a fetish.
Please, dip my pacifier in whiskey
I assure you I am not an alcoholic.
Please, bring your vagina over here
I assure you I am ready to leave.

Material Bomb

Someone told me
about my nightmares.
Said you could rarely feel them
but you'll feel them, boy,
when you write this book.

It wasn't a question of if
for him either.

And I wrote this book.

Brother and I

When we were children
we had to beg our father
to stay awake while driving
as mother's head lolled,
her hair burning in
oncoming headlights.

If we made it home
we could see inside the house
before opening the door,
not through the windows but
through a hole in the wall
where my father's fist
had splintered through
on a different raging night—
a big farmer's fist
bleeding wooden shards.

And sometimes
when they fought
I'd go to different holes
in the bedroom walls,
holes that were stuffed
with wet towels,
and scream
until I saw maudlin stars.

Wishing that something
from a different dimension
could hear through the
different medium,
through those wet towels
like spiritual curtains
I imagined waving
in that somewhere else
like pure sails over the
bluest sea.

Wishing that my voice
would spread like electricity
through that sea,
but I may as well have been yelling
into tampons,
into the womb's exit
where we were closed in,
where fate existed
no matter what my brother and I believed in.

Easing Time by Taking It Away

I awake on top of covers
still drunk, clothed,
lights on. My father
bursts through the door.
Time to get up,
he says, Come on
now. I crack my eyes,
red slits. He lingers,
walks out but doesn't
close the door;
with the laughter of my nephews
streaming in, my eyes roll back.
Later, I see them practicing
with fishing poles in the backyard.
Can't catch a trout in the grass,
I say, Don't let them see you—
they'll call you *crazy*!
My nephews laugh hard
and I feel something
similar to good,
lean against the fence
and look at weeds until
my father's shadow consumes
the afternoon sun.
Don't you think it's time
to slow down, he says.
How'd those dandelions
get so tall, I ask.
Don't change
the subject, he says
as we saunter
back to the house
languid as if under the ocean.

Middle of the Lake

A male friend calls me, crying
because a woman left, found out
that he cheated. He's one of my best
so I hear it. He's sorry
and so am I.

Then another friend calls, complaining
about work. The boss did this,
he had to do that.

Don't these people realize
that I'm two sips from being a bum?

And my brother, that son of a bitch,
all he does is talk about the job, caught
in some kind of muck like the rest,
going down narrow channels in the river
trying to get somewhere.

But for me, everything is wide open here.
I plan to sift through this lake until—
until, *ah shit*, until a great blue heron
takes me away.

I did, however, almost try to get a tan today
for a woman I can't keep,
only lasted five minutes, between the neighbors'
humored faces and sweat stinging my eyes:
I shall be a pale white man for as long as I can,
though I love you all,
who of you can blame me
for staying in this contained body of water, brimming
until the flood?

This Mourning Dove

In every room there is no room for art.
Voices stream from boxes, images of
American absurdity.
My father, estranged, sardonically yells:
"Someone took the batteries out of the remote!
Some body, ah-hee-he-heee!"
And my mother speeds about, eagerly,
room to room: "I can't find my glasses
if I can't see them!"

I take my blue notebook to the backyard.
It's so bright and stifling that it feels like I'm shitting,
pushing this thing out on the sun.

The neighbor is a
radio full of announcements
flag whipping in the caustic breeze
motorcycle revving engine
man going through the 45 yr. old plunge
trying to make as much noise as possible to keep
from thinking, the American way
a goblet overflowing with beer
"I'm only having four, honey!"

And the train shoots by
at the foot of this lawn,
jostling, clamoring
along rails, screeching
breaks, honking that horn.

Don't these people know that I'm a, uh—
what was I?

A mourning dove quietly lands on the deck banister,
sick with fear of human hullabaloo,
feathers ruffled, tipping into a mindless darkness

it looks at me with small, wet black eyes,
blinks rapidly, shits one tiny black pebble
like a burnt piece of gravel, then
flies off and drops dead
in the babel air.

These flames
burning my skin
I now know
that we are sweat
blotching about the paper
erasing our own
words.

The Salesman

All day
I hear my father working in the basement
talking loudly into a speakerphone
his voice drifting up and deep
through the vents.

At night, the strange thing night,
as he sleeps I hear his swivel chair, absent of him but
its wheels still scratching below
chipping the basement's painted floor—
the chair turning circles
and rising like a helicopter blade
into my dreams,
his bald scalp lying in the seat's center and
glowing like a moon, which, even upon waking
I never escape.

My Old Man

My father liked to pretend gruff and hearty
growing up on a farm with big hands,
lean lanky muscles that turned into beefy limbs
and a milk barrel waist.
The day you became weak, father,
was when you were finally all grown up
and decided to stay Christian because
it's taught. The day you went hunting
though the fridge was full of food
and you cried over killing a beautiful deer
because you just wanted to run with the pack.
The day a small bat flew in your hair
and you drowned it in a milk jug, later
bragging about its fate to children as if it were truly a vampire,
as if you were truly a slayer
and not just an impressionable rind
stifling in the surrounding herd of the good farm fields
not noticing the soil grow darker
the more you dug the ordinary man.
And still today you take me fishing
and scrutinize me for not putting my hook
deep in the fish's gullet
for fun.
I sit in this boat now
watching you bob with the river,
waiting for the line to tug
so you can simply say you stuck a fish
only to throw it back
and I wonder, is it the sun
that turns your face so red
or the reflection of autumn leaves
falling about your softened head.

Material Bomb

My mother has been winding me for years
with solitude and sandwich spread,
a car in her name that I can't drive
and a Huffy bike that pedals like boulders roll uphill.

I decided to stay put, you see,
pen and paper, pen and paper, pen and
drink and smoke pen and paper.

But not leaving the house
doesn't give me much to write about
except her and dad.

Last night, at the camper,
just as meteors showered down like ghostly suns
lighting the tree-shadowed park, my mother turned
with green wine dribbling down her chins
and sneered, "The bitch is back!"

You see, she found something I wrote
about her, and now I will never
hear the end.

Today she asked when my
New York Quarterly publication
is coming out. There's a poem
about my father in there. My success
at tearing family members apart
with the written word
and sitting like a toothless mute
when I should be venting
with verbal backlash
is becoming more and more apparent
as I think about how mom
owns the car I can't drive,
but dad

27

owns the roof over my head,
and all the things I'll see
living on the street,
like those ghostly suns
hitting Earth...

Boom, boom.

Boom.

My Mother

A vagina pumping oil
like suction-cups climb walls.

Two fingers walking
across a page and
jumping off.

A warm
makeup smeared telephone
dial tone.

Self-help
anxiety cassettes
fast-forwarding.

Pills rattling
in the vents.

Noodles boiling
to mush.

Unwashed clothes
in the washing machine
for days.

The screeching turntable
of a microwave
and a trail of balled kleenex
leading to the bedroom.

In a Fresh Cotton T

My little nephew is fat.
When he eats he breathes deep
between bites, like someone
between sexual strokes.
It disgusts me. I know
I'm not supposed to state it.
Disgusts me.

He
licks goobers
from his crusted
upper lip.

My other little nephew is Autistic.
But that's no excuse for ass picking,
penis twaddling
in his undies.

He
never wears pants when home.
Sometimes doesn't change his underwear
for days. Need I state it?
Disgusts me.

Their mother shits with the bathroom door open.
She's pretty, but I imagine
her poop is vile as my brother's
nervy stool.

Sometimes when I get done visiting
I feel like I've been soaking in a jar
of lint filled jelly.

Sticky,
I take lots of showers
and when someone asks:
Why aren't you married?
or
Why don't you have kids?

I feel clean.

Everybody's Always Talking about God

My brother complains
that his wife cheats on him
and dresses him
like a fag.

He's smoked
so many cigarettes
that they've prescribed him
plastic ones.

Last night, by mistake,
at 3 a.m. he sent me this
text message:

U don't know shit
about me fucken
my wife was a big
mistake. Big
mistake. I WILL
SEE U.

And now, while we sit around a campfire,
his son drags over a branch, drops it
quickly out of fright and
wipes little bugs off his forearms.

Throw it in the fire, my brother says.

But there's bugs on it, his son says.

So what? They're just bugs, my brother says.

Carefully, with just his fingertips,
his son picks up the branch and holds it outward
then tosses it into the fire,

sending out a storm of sparks
that momentarily light our eyes like fireflies.

The bugs on the branch
pop, smoke, and sizzle
like small, insignificant things
burning alive, music
when I say, *You just lost
your right to
complain of
God, God, God, God, God.*

A Poem You May Want To Reread

My brother's wife
talks a lot of dumb shit.

What are those things called, she says,
I like them. It starts with a 'P.'

Peanuts? I say.

No, no, they're flowers. Um...
Peonies, she yells, *I like peonies!*

Oh, mmm, I say.

I like white peonies the best.

I look at my Caucasian brother,
wink.

But I've had a lot of peonies,
red, yellow, and black peonies...

My brother frowns.
It's known to be true.

When she says peonies it sounds
so much like an oriental trying to say penis
that I can't help but put the word in her mouth
and the conversation actually feels quite lively.

I love peonies! she says
while I grin and nod
and my brother twists
his wedding ring.

It's known to be true.

34

Divorce

Darkness is laid out on my brother's couch,
eyes wide to the ceiling, listening to the house's guts.
Children are asleep upstairs. Their fists beat the walls in dreamy anger.
I am alone downstairs. The toilet chuffs and gargles,
chuffs and gargles—I turn to it and imagine a ghost
plunging its invisible shit—a real hell that I stop by jittering the handle.
What they call dead noise. Silence brings peace, but that's a lie.
The red, dirty panties of my brother's wife are lying on the floor
in the shape of smiling lips. They are excited,
too much so, belonging to a woman during divorce.
They are caked like a white topped tongue, hard with pleasure.
Something has been happening, says the smell of beluga caviar
and the computer full of bearded men.
The walls moan and scratch with what they've seen,
paintings of nude women clawing floors,
the wife's abstract lust. I look and think
and I feel it growing all around me
as the red-eyed guinea pig watches, licking its paws
and stroking its fur
before the children wake to school.

The First Time Snakes Ever Battled on Ice

We timed it so
we would plummet
together, the arctic hill
cut by our sleds,
its snow like skin-flakes
flying into our eyes,
I saw red and
swear there were
hulking beasts
that grinned and pulled us
quicker down,
just as spirits of liquor
in plagued minds do:
my mind, my brother's mind—
and when I veered into my brother's path
to stiff-arm him, he was quick
with a blow to my chest
that sent us both reeling
off our sleds,
twisting in the snow together,
locked like serpents
deciding just who the king cobra was,
going down, down.

Muenster Cheese

At the Chinese restaurant
a placemat tells me
I was a rat in a past life.

My brother a snake.
My dad a goat.
My grandpa a dragon.
My mother a cock.

Fitting. But a rat?
A furtive, afraid rodent
that thrives in dark holes?
Well...perhaps, definitely
after discovering on the news
that rats recover all brain cells
when taking a break
from alcohol addiction.

There is hope, I tell myself
while standing before a mirror
and twisting the long whiskers
surrounding my human mouth.

American Eagles, 2009

After thirty hours of pounding
my father's heart finally exploded
in a snow storm.
Almost a year passed and grandma
still wasn't over it
so I took her by the Eagle Center
to keep her mind off
things. It was a wet autumn drive, the leaves falling
like confetti. One sad story after another
the whole way there, about her brother
not being able-minded enough
to visit this year. About how he was
always talking to God in cornfields, waving fists
at the sky, and how after all this time he finally got it in his head
that he, himself, was God.
Now the dope has him.
Then she told about her other brother, the mildly sane one,
and the saddest sight she ever did see—him
crying as his barn burned, the cows howling
like spirits on fire, and the cats
turned to cinders running out
with their eyes bubbling.
Her brother had to hit them with the hammer.
And oh God her dad died
the same age as Jesus Christ under a bulldozer.
But I couldn't
get the picture of my own father out of my head,
him lying in the snow, hand over heart
as if pledging the allegiance.
By the time we arrived at the Eagle Center
I was almost dripping like the autumn trees.
I barely managed to get a hold of myself and steady grandma,
her cane an extra, worthless limb.
I can't get health insurance, she said.
It's kind of ironic, she said, that whenever I apply for it
I am always denied by someone young and healthy.

The Eagle Center was large and full
of children. Automated machines
told us facts: Eagles can see pigeon wings flap
from four miles away.
We were handed pamphlets
and I had to read them to Grandma, her eyesight
neither far nor near.
Eagle wings span up to seven feet.
Grandma was noticeably shorter this year
like each month was a tiny stair downward.
Eagles are hard of hearing. That they had in common.
What? she said. Eagles are hard of hearing, I said, g'damnit.
An eagle flew around a wooden display
and the tour guide said it'd probably live another thirty years.
Grandma a year from eighty, I asked if she wanted her picture taken
next to that eagle.
She shuffled, limped over.
The eagle, tethered to the guide's arm, watched intently
with its constant glare.
Grandma stood a foot away, well within reach,
and the eagle continued to study her with its sharp eyes, its head bobbing
forward, some kind of high-pitched jeers
coming from its open maw.
It tasted the air with its tongue
like some perverted thing
salivating for rare, old meat.
The room filled with anticipating children
who were taught that eagles preyed on the weak,
the wounded and the old.
For a moment I saw it from grandma's perspective,
the faces of the children that surrounded her
all a big blur of teeth—
She forced a denture smile
unaware of what they wanted
as the eagle spread its talons
and rose like some demonic angel,

its wings blowing the hair away from all the youngsters' eyes.
One, the camera man said.
I waited for the attack.
Two, the camera man said.
To be followed by stifled laughter.
Three, the camera man said.
The American way—
Flash.

Cheers Ladies

I'm a miserable guest
when at the nursing home
visiting grandma.
It takes two vodka tonics
no room for limes
prior to leaving
before I can even attempt a smirk
in that place.
It's not the peoples' fault
I keep telling myself, sadness
isn't their invention,
nor is cruelty, pain or
loopy happiness. But the last time I was there
the nicest looking little old lady
called me a Skank
in the most vile voice
that can only come from such aged corrosion.
Me—a Skank! With my dented bald head
and vodka breath. Well,
maybe she was right, maybe
I was whoring myself to bring grandma
a little love, all the while putting up with
another lady named Beth
making me beaded necklaces,
and old Susie across the table
her memory kaput, eighty thinking she's nineteen
trying to play footsy in purple socks,
arching her eyebrows
and twirling the hairs in her ears,
a smirk and a wink from my glassed-over eyes.

To See What Happens

Grandma believed in heaven and hell
so thoroughly that in the years before she died
she thought she was going to hell
and that someone was coming to take her there.

Black dogs circling the house,
gas through the vents,
poison food.
The congregation's hate,
the sermon's hunt,
damnation by candle fire,
the devil knows.

She had a stroke thinking about it.

And dad had been considering death
since his heart attack, but seemed to crawl
farther from religion after the horror
of his mother.

Crawling, crawling, crawling
even after our dog died
put to sleep due to cancer.

Slowly gaining distance
only holding onto prayer,
my parents drove home
with our dog in a shoebox.

My mom came inside,
her sunglasses
dripping like faucets.

Outside, dad popped the trunk,
walked around to the back of the car
and hid behind it.

Watching from the bay window
I asked mom, "What's he doing
behind that trunk?"

From the screen-door
she could see him.

"He's looking at the body," she said.

And I pictured him slowly opening the shoebox,
then staring down at our dog's lifeless
brown eyes.

Dad closed the trunk, grabbed the shovel
and the rock headstone.

Through an open window
I listened to him dig
but didn't watch that.

And always
I've wanted to ask,
never to actually
ask, "Why'd yuh look
in the box, pa?"

*Why'd   yuh   look
in   the   box?*

Up and Down

My father walks around outside
opening and closing all the car doors
repeatedly,
checking under the boat's tarp,
and pushing on the shed
to make sure it doesn't fall off
its stone blocks.

My father has been very
burdened
since his mother entered the
psych ward
for thinking children were coming to
kill her,
among other shadows, and trying to
kill herself.

My father walks around the house
opening and closing all the bedroom doors
whether we're asleep or not,
slamming cupboards
and pulling the fridge apart,
keeping everyone awake.

Up and down
fidgeting, lousy,
sleeping pills and vodka
but up before sunrise
regardless.

It isn't all right, pa,
but it's going to be, pa, all
right???

It's in My Blood

It's true
religion made my grandma crazy.
Ask a religious fanatic who
thinks they're going to hell
how much they read the bible.
Combine that with a deteriorating mind
and you've got my grandma's
delusions in a psych ward.

It must be said though she had
guts
to bust the glass picture on the wall
with her fist
and hold a shard to her neck
demanding
they let her out of the nursing home,
thus getting herself put in
the psych ward (which was
actually much quieter
and less full
of death).

But still
it's all fucked up.
I know some religious people
are going to attack me
for being agnostic and
writing poems like this,
but when asking
why I'm not religious
please recall
where I came from,
as I'll recall
the black hounds frothing at the mouth
that supposedly circled my grandma's house
or the poison that peppered her food

or the congregation that was coming
to murder her, her mind already in
hell
before any afterlife,
demons seeping
from the pockets of her visitors
in the locked-down psych ward.

And if you must
still give *me*
hell about it
go ahead.
It runs in the
family—

My own father thought
the devil lived in our attic.
My own uncle thought
he was God.

Me? Shit
I just write poems.

But My Sunshine Is Brighter Than Hers

Stay inside for weeks, don't leave
the house. Do this for years.
Then take a few hours to go visit
your grandma in the psych ward.
Let that be your sunshine, writer.
Repeat. And when they come
to visit you in your little bedroom, ask
them how it smells. They'll
let you know
because they're your friends.

Pendulum Eyes

I'm in Wisconsin
sharing the sun
with China,
waiting for it to rise
on my side.

We're all overcome
by darkness
—a dash of navy paint
on a black canvas—
but tonight if
I knew their Chinese tongue
I'd be desperate enough
to demand   to scream   to say calmly as possible, quivering:
Give me back the
sun.

Childless

I must be a negative person
because I often wonder why
I was brought into this world,
why *I* must suffer it.

How pompous to think
another person would want
to be here, and then stick your pecker
in its mother, leaving it
no choice.

I must've been one of your
stupid sperms, unknowing that
it'd evolve to this—the heart
in my neck and feet
far too strong and rapid
as if I am bleeding out
inside.

I crack an egg
over the stove
and watch it sizzle,
no expectations
to be made,
not even to
continue on.

I'm simply hungry.

Selling the House

Someday there might be
a knock on your door,
and then a visitor will leave.
And there'll be another
knock on your door—
a different visitor with
the same inquiry
as the last. This will continue
until you, yourself, and yours
are gone from the house,
and it'll probably continue
even after that. These strange visitors
asking to see the room
where the young man lived
all his life.

My Death

My death is Mayfly's
many night old novels
flapping under streetlights.

My death is drums
beat with heron beaks
while floating down
Mississippi channels.

My death is ant wars
on anteater tongues
slurped into guts.

My death is classic
mushroom cloud beauty
illuminating black oceans.

My death is moon
falling slowly to earth
in deafening silence.

My death is Jupiter
speaking,
its red eye
looking.

My death is Milky Way
spilling down God's throat.

My death is
universe.

Let's Save Ourselves

Life isn't
a life saver.

Sometimes
it's like riding
a raft in the middle
of the ocean
where down below
only sharks.

Sometimes
the raft pops.

It's bound to happen
with all those teeth
constantly gnawing.

And you won't
always be thrown
a buoy.

Sometimes
you have to swim
until you find
someone else's
raft, someone else
who is willing
to help.

And that
in itself
can kill you
when realizing
just how
alone
you
are.

But if you
find yourself
sinking
at the time
you read this
poem
please
don't
let yourself
die:

Ride
that motherfucking
shark
to your
own
little island
your
own
little beach
and
be content
with yourself
and the fact
that life
isn't
a life saver.

Trust me.
I've been there.
I've swelled the eyes
of many a shark
and sometimes
just barely
I wash upon
the shore

and it is
marvelous
to have
survived.

Fight.

Be a
Man.

Be a
Woman.

And know
that there is
no
person
on earth
that can judge
you.

And know
that though
most
people
are cold
and
uncaring
that I
and
people
like me
are out there.

I
will always
let you
on my
raft.

Let us
float
upon
the words.

Let us
be
content
alone
and
not
so
alone.

We
are
beautifully
kicking
to
shore.

Love Winter

---

*I don't need to jog
to exercise my heart,
I just need to watch
my chest's shadow
beating the wall
reciting her poems.*

But Somehow It Does

A black beauty in a bikini
circles my neighbor's house
and is gently led inside
by his hand.

A week later
comes a petite brunette,
and after her a blonde
that I'd wear a diaper to
suck the nipples of,
dignity out the door.

All these women I watch
watering his manicured lawn,
bending, sometimes getting on hands and knees
to fondle his flowers,
windows of his big house
holding a perfect afternoon glare
so no one can see what happens
when he leads them inside,
past his SUV's twenty-two-inch rims
lined perfectly with his boat.

And here I am
living in my parents' window
with nothing but paper
and a sad dick,
contemplating the dream I had
where I was a horse with a broken leg
kicking myself away from a forthcoming
crowd of leering people,
mane dripping with an oily substance
polluted with fear,
right between life and death,
indecisive to which is better.

No, I'm not mad
at my neighbor
or even bitter
about my current situation
and the dream that left me
shaking on the toilet.

I'm only dumbfounded
at how completely different
lives can be.

Then I go to the computer
and jerk off to a black beauty,
a brunette, and a blonde.

When all done
I glance at his house
one last time
before closing the blinds,
thinking
our lives aren't so different.

And wouldn't you know it?
Over the radio comes news
of more innocent bystanders
     ex-plo-ding
but it doesn't matter to anyone
at a continent's distance
except those alone long enough
to consider it.

What's So Funny?

By the time I arrived I had finished
a quart of orange juice and vodka.
It was a ten-hour drive to my friend's house
near the burned down streets of Detroit,
the first place I had ever really
felt like a minority,
my pale skin a candle.
It was me: the drunk, single, childless man,
and my friend, his wife, his kids,
and my brother, his wife, his kids.
Needless to say the kids
thought it strange
how flames reflected in my eyeglasses.

The first night my brother and my friend were to watch
the children,
while I went bar hopping
with the wives.
"To make sure there isn't any trouble," I said
and by the end of the night
I had grabbed both the wives'
asses. I remember on the way back
chasing my brother's wife with my cupped hands out,
laughing like the moon.
When I saw my brother standing on the front steps
I stopped like the moon
at midnight as black clouds of shame drifted by.
"I still love her," he told me later.
"Oh," I said. "I thought you didn't."

The next morning
everyone seemed in good enough spirits
except me.
I had spent the night at my friend's house
and felt like a sheep.
When I saw his wife, she handed me a pink towel

to shower with, said she tried to find one more manly.
"I'll dry off fast," I said.
There is no deeper shame
than shame when you're hungover.
All through lunch I stared at my food
thinking I was drinking the children's breast milk.
Then I started drinking the hard stuff
and it was okay again.

We went to the Henry Ford museum
and I stared at black schoolgirls in the Rosa Parks bus.
Imagined some of their panties were lace
but most were cotton. Clean white
cotton overlapping immaculate lips.
Later that night I was told
to sleep in my friend's daughter's room
while she slept in her little brother's.
Her jeans were lying on the floor and of course
cotton panties were stuffed inside.
I couldn't help myself. Picked them up. They
looked clean, something clean that had covered
something clean, and I thought I'd never smell
something that fresh, so I did.
It smelt faintly of urine
and bubblegum.

When the sun rose to noon it started all over,
my sheepish ways.
To make it even worse I had rolled over on my glasses
and could barely see.
My friend's wife tried to fix them,
held them above my face while I was lying down,
her lips hovering over mine, looking into my eyes...
I thought she was going to kiss me for a second!
What a laugh!
A bad, bad laugh.

But somewhat natural, a lust.
I hope you turn red
remembering your own lusts.

During the drive back home
I almost puked. Going by Chicago
there was a woman painted on the side of a building
playing piano and silently singing.
She was pretty, immaculate too.
I took a picture of me and my little nephew,
his head on my shoulder. He looked
like he was about to cry. I looked
crazy with my eyebrow cocked, eyes so glassy
that when the camera flashed
it was as if the light ate my pupils and my insides.

But even after all that had happened
the memory of the trip that sticks in my head
every time I see that picture
is of my brother, his wife, my friend, and his wife—
all their faces laughing about something
around the kitchen table,
teeth and lips purple with wine.

Crazy, In My Dream

Walking along a red sidewalk,
even red in my peripheral, but a calm
red like a setting sun as I focused
on the sidewalk's cracks and your
small brown feet, nails painted
red. It was a nice languor,
loving. I asked you to be my girl
and you hesitated, but finally said
Yes. Really? I said. Yes, you said
and I felt that red flowing through my chest
at ease, sighing with it. My cheeks grew
weary with smile. We went hand in hand
to the restaurant, leaned
on the counter to order,
when a man came in with a knife,
jaundice eyes yellow amid his blackness.
He saw you and grabbed you and pushed
the knife below your chin. But you didn't scream.
Didn't have time because I pulled him back,
flipped the knife and tore it through the underside of his wrist,
stabbed him over and over and over, undeterred
by *his* mercy screams. The knife would only go
half an inch through his meat, as if it were
too tough. So I kept stabbing, then finally
gave up. Left him there, squirming in his own red.
A vibrant red. An angry red and
I awoke. You weren't there.
Didn't even exist. I'd been single
for years. Still was. But in that dream
it really felt good to protect you.
My face is red with it
now. A somber red. Please
come home.

Satan Says, Daughter Revisited

I want to fuck Sharon Olds's mind,
that mind sucking on my cock.

I want to combine us and
do it in front of her alcoholic father,
German but sick as an Auschwitz Jew
while she writes it all down.

Fireplace shining through a glass of bourbon
flickering auburn about the walls.

Satan says, *Sharon Olds*
get down on your knees.

Enter the choir of blind girls.
All heard is the slurping
between verses of Little Drummer Boy.

Satan says, *Give them sight.*
Pa, rum-pum-pum—pum.

Outside, the wind rises,
sounds like a sudden heavy rain
of babies.

A newborn king to see.
Pa, rum-pum-pum—pum.

The man of Sharon's night terrors,
short as Picasso and just as broad,
dances naked circles around us,
his hair black as a polished stove pipe
but bouncing like a wind feather.

Les Demoiselles d'Avignon comes to life
and forms a twisted merry-go-round,

faces rounded shards. Picasso, revisited—
my masterpiece.

Satan scratches devil pubes.
The earth cracks, he says,
and people fall in.

Babies slip through the ceiling and
their bodies slap the hardwood floor
like six pound steaks.

They morph into wounded soldiers on cots,
moan.

Come, they tell me.
Pa, rum-pum-pum—pum.

Sharon's pointed breasts turn heavy
with spermy milk.

Out of the fireplace, Sharon's mother crawls
naked and charred. Languid
the mother pulls a shriveled ovary out of her caustic cut,
carries it cupped in her hands, lightly stepping
nearer, nearer.

Rub it in the cum, Satan says,
be a swallower.

Sharon takes the ovary, rolls it around her white nipples,
pushes it down her throat, swallows it whole.
The bulge slips down her neck.

The father weeps and
the mother drops to the floor,
convulses and spreads her legs

until the father jumps inside
the cut. Disappears.

A drunk republican stumbles out of the fireplace
now, the only way he can get his kicks
without the dollar bill; he tackles Sharon,
pounds his fists into her belly
to murder, to murder.

Stomp him,
Satan says.

And I turn the republican into burnt
mushy flakes
stuck to the bottom of my boot.

Sharon screams, stands and clutches
her belly. A stillborn baby dangles
upside down between her legs.

But the blood pulses in its deformed head.

Our finest gifts we bring.
Pa, rum-pum-pum—pum.

Sharon's mother arches on the floor.
Her charred tits point at me
like two wicked eyes.
A woman bursts through her chest,
steps out of the heart, dripping.
Sharon's sister, beat,
scarred and prodded.

Take it, Satan says, *raise
it, give it
to the wife beater.*

The sister pulls the soft baby
from Sharon's crotch,
the sound of suction cup,
and sprints to the black, cold window,
leaps through the glass with our daughter
in her arms. Our baby.
To give it to the
Japanese frogman.

Spreading Literature

I want to open a woman's legs like a book,
flip through and sniff
then put them on a lighted shelf
where I can sit and admire their title
and when guests arrive I can say
that's my wife.

But if they try to slide her off the shelf
I don't want to get angry
as the married man,
I want to say Look here, what I found
is worth more than your time and
I'd like to share it with you.

For there is nothing more beautiful
than a great female author
no matter how musty your room is.

Look at the back page photograph
and know
no matter how single and pathetic lonely you are
that this woman's inner workings
are free.

Here, I want to whisper,
it's ours.

Digging Up Sexton

God is only mocked by believers!
—Anne Sexton

You're a massive book like the bible, now
dead, but lingering like a god—beautiful
as Jesus naked, levitating on a cross of lingerie,
your arms free and swooning
the universe, the bell between your legs
dank and sweet as a grape.
I kneel to place this poem at your feet
in all its glorious mockery,
in want of the bones you speak of so often
in your great book, imagining they are lunar as the moon
but smooth as newly pressed silverware.
I am the incestual Norman Bates
and you are my mother. Hooded
I go to your grave where the grass dances
like sequenced swimmers, the surroundings
of your marker a macabre, surreal cartoon,
Jim Morrison sitting atop it, kicking his feet
and running fingers through the engravings
of your name—he sings *Oh show me
the way   to the next   whiskey bar*—
Moby Dick laid out beneath a tree
sipping a martini and gurgling *Annie, Annie,
Annie* between bursts of deep whale laughter,
bubbles of blood popping into his eyes
while lavender butterflies blow fire
at birds in this Disney-ish world, sick
and gorgeously violent—a trans-
formation. I begin to dig
with all my might through the vibrant color
of your lot, green as the leaves in your head.
I want to have your virgin bones like Snow White
in a field of daisies, not yet picked by necrophiliacs,
the sky a blue eye, one of yours
like J.R.R. Tolkien's Mordor eye

shining your imagination upon me
with a great, piercing light, that of a play—us
at play. The deeper in your ground I get
the louder the witch voices become,
muffled but echoing from within your skull
like leaves, rocks, spit, whips and razors—
patients of the asylums moaning, roaming
the cemetery, lifting their nightgowns
and lashing at their privates to Moby Dick's
Annie, Annie, Annie. I lay down
and put my ear to the ground
where I think your face is below.
Acorns fall like anvils now
and the land spits mud.
At last my hands, sodden with dirt
reach your coffin and pry it open
with a fearful adrenaline.
The lid doesn't squeal, it sighs
with smoky breath, and there are
your remains, beautiful dark poet,
your skull white as toddler teeth
wearing the hat you were married in,
the deceiving color of virgin,
and your shirt spotted yellow
with every kitchen you ever painted.
I lift it over your head
and play a tune on your ribs
with your knuckles, remove
the black padded bra, the maternity skirt
and the teenage white cotton panties.
It is everything I ever hoped for! You—
untouched! They may have gotten
your flesh, but these bones—these bones
are as smooth as an elephant's baby tusks.

Excited, I linger and wave
over them like a pantomime.
Then I hear it, an interruption, a song
of dwarfs—*Hi ho!   Hi ho!   Off to work
we go!*—and there they are, plodding over
the hill, evil leers on their little fat mugs,
axes and pickaxes held high in the air
preparing to strike, Grumpy the sickest of all
in his red rags, and Dopey stumbling drunk
with blood on his face.
They have come to take you away from me,
with their seven fury cocks.
Moby Dick scoots away on his fins
and Jim Morrison runs into a bar across the street.
Your bright blue eye flutters between clouds
and my surroundings become a strobe light,
the dwarfs black as demon silhouettes.
I begin to weep and fondle your bones
for the first time, for the last time,
and there I discover, etched into your pelvis
Sylvia was here—
your skull turns with grinding teeth
and out of the sides of your jaw comes a voice
like burning crickets
*You will suffer
and it will be kind*[1]—
I hear a galloping
and begin to climb out of the grave
to escape, but my footing slips
and I am clutched by the arms, swept up
onto the back of a donkey,
the donkey you rode into death,
where I wrap my arms around

---

1   from *Letters to Dr. Y.*, June 6, 1967, by Anne Sexton

Sylvia Plath's cloaked waist.
I thought you were dead, I say.
Her head turns full circle
and I am faced with what seems to be a hollow
black hood, until her tongue
rolls into my ear, whispers
Daddy, Daddy I will keep you
moist—and like this, we ride off on death's donkey,
sniffling beneath my collar
like trench coat perverts.

I Carry It

Last night in my sleep
a massive female cousin
swung a knife at my face
while a large winged bug
squeezed into my ear.

-

I dream of falling in love

with women I knew only vaguely,
their mannerisms imprinted
in my lonely mind,
their saliva like honey
in my hair
dripping onto my hungry
out-stuck tongue

their lavender voices, their soft lips—

I hope you've known love
at least once,
but if you've fallen off the bridge
into deep, deep water
it will haunt you
not being able to swim.

-

Sometimes a ghost
caresses me in my sleep,
its fingertips
gossamer ash.

Sometimes I levitate
right through the covers,

74

the shadows of my room
bouncing to the abduction.

I awake on my side
paralyzed,
barely able to open my eyes
halfway, to turn slightly
shaking with fear
and see the outline of a black figure,
so black that nothingness would be jealous
sitting in bed next to me.

-

Sleep is a bitter serum
that drenches the sun.

I carry sleep like lizard skins,
I carry it like snake tongues
flicking into my eyes

and my head hurts.

Preach

Van Gogh's face covered in coal,
hunched with the shadows.
Eyes glowing yellow, sunk
beneath his blackened brow.
Ear but a blotch of red, heart
but a long stream of undrunk love
wrapping around your feet
he whispers, "Do not blame God
for the artist made this world
on one of his bad days
when wits weren't about him."

Thin Sliced, Moist Ham

There's a bum that I give money to
when drinking downtown. In the evening
he waits for the sandwich restaurant to
bring its day's worth of garbage out, still fresh.
He gets very excited, gleeful, tells me these
black bags are life savers, presents when you're starving,
says the leftover sandwiches have all fallen apart but
they can still be pieced together—
a little meat there, get that olive, get that cheese
but whatever you do, he says, don't look at the bite marks
or picture the real people who ate it:
fat fingers, dirty nails, bad breath, yellow teeth.
No, he says, forget them and
picture a beautiful blonde college girl,
tongue pink as her innards,
lips juicy as the tomato, then
it's not so bad
being a bum it's beautiful!

Love Winter

The street is prettier than the sky,
a fresh, thin sheet of snow
that glitters like millions of winking white
beluga whale eyes—

it falls around me

as I follow the black tracks
of shoes pointed at the toe
with the smell of her soft, cold skin
lingering over them and her liquor
coated lips   so kissable

and numbing.

The unseeable presence
of her love scooped in my hand
and crumbling out
like the smallest, velvet crystals—

it solidifies in my mind

like a lustful hug
as I come to the spot
where her shoes pivoted
and she turned full circle
to peer at her follower—

a lone glove on ice.

Is it one of hers?
I sniff it and
write on a windshield:

love winter.

The Little Geniuses That They Might Be

I met a woman, ma. Remember
I said it'd happen one of three ways:
a poetry reading, a whiskey, or a letter…
Well, she came one and a half of the ways:
a letter saying how she liked my poetry.
She's very smart, has me busting out
the dictionary…is going to school
for Philosophy and Criminal Justice.
Only lives a few miles away! But
I told her I'm not ready. And
it's true. Told her about my social anxiety
and how the doctor recently prescribed
Prozac and Lorazepam. And get this:
she's on Prozac and Lorazepam too!
I never thought I'd be so happy
to hear of someone else's dysfunctions.
Not only that, she has Obsessive Compulsive Disorder,
Bulimia and Hypochondria—but I believe
it's under control, judging by her letters
anyhow. The medication seems to be working.
Besides, the amount of anxiety I have
probably equals all her problems
balled into one. And I told her
I'm unemployed, but she doesn't mind.
As long as I'm going to get a job,
she says. She believes in my writing
too. And her brother has Autism
just like my nephew! We have
so much in common, ma…
she says her ma pees her pants
when she laughs too hard too!
Don't laugh about it, ma, please.
Anyway, I'm trying to get my life
together, see. I hope it works out
with this girl. I really do.
She even says she wants to write

memoirs. Memoirs, ma! How great
is that? Also, I told her that I might
live in a tent on the Mississippi
islands for a whole summer,
seeing as I can eat fish
rent free, and then I'll have time
to write my first book. She
doesn't mind that either…
even says she might come with me
to write her own book! We
are so fucked up—and great.
That's what it takes to be great,
ma, you gotta be a little crazy,
got it? *Zumbubaloobah!*
In her last letter she said
she missed her period, and she's scared
that it's a sign she has some disease.
That's the Hypochondria, ma.
She's not having sex. We're
not having sex, yet, but I told her
that I'd make her miss her period
for real, and she says she hopes
I do. Just think of that, ma!
This girl might be the mother
of my children! Imagine that…
Just imagine your grandchildren, ma.

You've Had Enough

You come home
from a bad day—a bad year—a
bad decade
and find a boy not yours
chasing your daughter.
Grab-assing around the house, throwing pillows,
the air filled with feathers
slowly falling.
You recognize his laugh
from across the room, from the times
your daughter whispered to him over the telephone
and he laughed so loud he
rattled the receiver. The boy, hounding
your daughter with playful lusts
but she likes it
through the feathers of your soft
personal family pillows, now
torn to bits.
You see skins and
squeeze the bottle, raise it
high above your head
until it bursts from your grip
much more than wine red.
It sprinkles before your eyes,
dribbles down your head, settles
in your ears, drowns the drums.
"Daddy?" your daughter calls,
"Daddy!" You've
had enough,
when just in time
a long ago memory comes back—
Rojean, your former *untouched*
soon to be touched teenage love, the one
you referred to as *flesh petals*
with your tongue
and the nights you were happy and young—

81

Now, old man, it's simple:
swallow your saliva
toss them a condom
turn around
open the front door
and walk out.
But your daughter follows
and calls to you again.
You roll down the car window,
say, "Have at it,"
before driving off
with hopes that she'll go back inside
and do as you wish.

Affix

She's intangible, but there
in my head again. This time
I won't push her away, instead
cup her in my hands like a fish
dying on land. I shall move gingerly
and make absolute so that
no love spills from my fingers
and takes her air away.
This may be a folly, for I too
am a fish, cupped in her hands,
one that she may grow weary of
carrying, and set down in the prickly grass
where I will spit my last drops of air
at the sun. All similes aside, girlie,
do you know my first waking thought today?
Tea. Iced tea. Second thought:
Nikki. Eventually you will replace thirst.
You will be the river that mankind settled next to
in order to survive. This is no joke.
People have died in droughts. We are not
just a metaphor. Me and you
are real.

Ending Our Relationship

All these roads I want
to cover with dirt, travel
by horse, Eastwood scowl
in the middle of eighteen
chimpanzees riding ponies
and grinding cigars
with yellow teeth,
red eyes glaring like Mars
amongst all that black fur,
my chest open to the sun
before I find her
and do the snake thing
coil
coil
share the bottle with my clan
then let the eighteen have their way
with her all at once,
gang ape rape while I stand
outside, back to the window,
moon grinning retarded down on me,
screams beating my drums, stroking
my black horse; a tear trickles
into the corner of my mouth
and I swallow it like vodka, cringe,
mount and ride off next to the daffy monkeys
jumping with the footfalls of their ponies.

See you around
girlie.

Missing Head

The cracked, headless torso
stands erect on a pedestal,
arms gone, legs gone,
but hip in place
with half a shattered penis.

The other half is lying on the floor
like a dildo gone hurtfully wrong,
reverberating clit pain.

And my brother's wife
decides this the appropriate time
to discuss why I haven't
been getting dates.

In All Seriousness

I was walking
under a stupid moon
that allowed me to see
to the left of a
grocery store's entrance
a lone college boy
humping a pumpkin.

Suddenly the moon
wasn't so stupid
and I was
a genius.

As for
that poor pumpkin,
it'd never see
Halloween.

This Man

This man, he rises at noon.
Sometimes not until two in the afternoon.
He drinks orange juice right away.
Makes a small meal, his favorite,
just big enough to soak up the *Casillero
del Diablo* leftover in his stomach.
He scoops lint out of his belly button.
Flicks it where he pleases.
Shirtless, he moves about slowly.
The heat just right. No use for pants.
He has a decent looking, smart woman
that believes in everything he does.
Sleeps till noon, too, and works evenings
while he writes, all the while believing.
And she doesn't smoke. Has smooth,
smooth legs. Stays in shape.
All she asks is that he eats her out
now and then. He doesn't mind.
She smells like coconut. Leaves
the scent all over him. This man
can smell her always. Sniffs himself.
Cleans the house with music
while she's away, works out, writes
then fucks her as long as he can
when she comes home. They're in love.
I'm in love just thinking about it.
This man, I want to be
this man!

Horripilation

---

*Down in the dirt
they don't let you breathe.
You have to wait until
the mortars drop and
bust you out.*

Absorb

I thought of novels
before I had the ability to write them
but saw their scenes in my head
like a movie theater made of bone,
and though I may never write them
the experience was beautiful,
a show made just for me
with my own private actors,
where none of the blood
was fake, where all the sex
was real, where women and children
died like men   and lived forever
in that moment   just like now
with the breeze
bringing curtains to brush my cheeks,
with the carpet
orange as flames cushioning my feet,
where I am alive
poised forever
over this keyboard,
fingers striking the black keys
then falling onto them
to absorb their heat
like a child's fevered temple.

Tonight My Muse Is Mexican

Dark messy, balding hair,
pillow muffled laughter—
Kill me, he says
as I shove his head
down harder into the soft
whiteness. Hard as I can.
His fists beat the mattress
with giggles; his feet kick
the strength from my arms
and I let go. He turns
over under me,
crazy with whiskers
and a wide, crooked grin.
I smash his nose
with my palm, make
bone infiltrate brain.
Ha! Ha! Ha! he laughs,
blood streaming from his nostrils,
red mires between his teeth.
Haw! Ha! I twist
his neck all the way around
and back, over and over,
crackle-crackle-crackle
his neck grows thinner
each time, taller like
it's made of clay;
his mangled face
looms, floats above
me in the moonlight
and his dry, rough tongue
rolls out, licks words
across my eyes: *Sí,*
escribir esto.

Historic Dreams

The sound of stars in my sleep.
It was a burning.
I was a black man
and their radiance hurt me,
kept me from fountains and diners,
hung me from looming trees.
My life was the night sky
and they were holes in it
piercing me with their lunar skin.
I began to sway, to rock, to circle,
and looking down I saw my long body
flickering orange, being poked
with sticks carved to spears.
They were checking to see if I was done.
Well done, boy, one man said
to a child sitting on his shoulders
singing *Twinkle   twinkle   little   star*
and I felt the burning rise from my torso,
the flames growing bigger with their wood.
My arms stretched above my head, tied
to a thick branch, my hairless pits
shaking. I hung.
Their faces luminous, so bright
that I could no longer see the sky
and my brothers didn't exist.
The last image being the little boy
high on the grinning man's shoulders,
his small feet
kicking excitedly.

When I woke up
I was a star.
Always had been,
except in the dreams
I knew sort of what it was like
to be black in history

and I knew all of what it was like
to be white now, to be
a star trying to beg the sky's forgiveness
by sharing fountains…diners…toilets.

Even though I was white
I wanted revenge for my dream self
and set out in a pointed hood
to find the clan that remained.
I gathered them in a basement for a meeting,
set them all to flames.
Turned them into a galaxy
so that I might see the space of my brothers.

Now, I am satisfied
and sleep has no color.
I eat with them all in diners,
say cheers with shared soda,
the sound of the fizz drowning out memories,
the caffeine keeping our hearts bumping
away from historic dreams.

But somewhere   I am scared.
Somewhere   I know what it was like.
Somewhere   little white feet
kick excitedly.

Viking Past, and Present Nostalgia

We rumbled Europe for two-hundred years—
we were a sign predicted in the bible of the
approaching end of the world.
Out of the north an evil
shall break forth.

        My brother and I are a known menace
        in downtown La Crosse.
        I watch my brother's glare
        in the barroom mirror.
        We are drinking to kill
        our minds.

Starting by destroying God's church
in Lindisfarne, we drowned the civilians
and stomped them with our polluted feet.
We were berserkers, chewing our shields,
tripping drunk with no prospects of finding wives or places to live,
for to preserve our sons we left our daughters
in the wild to die.

        My brother's fist dents the bar
        and sends ashes into the smoky air.
        "I want to fuck somebody up!"
        he shows me his teeth
        coated in whiskey.

We were villainous armies with nothing
to lose but our wintry souls to the beautiful Valkyrie.
We were Vikings. Sea kings
with only room on board our longships for weapons and drink—
Wicingas Kynn, Kin To The Pirates.

        The bartender is nervous,
        wiping glasses and glancing at us.
        The women are afraid;

their men hold onto them
like bows.

Dragon heads snarled from the heads of our ships
as we searched for clouds in the horizon—signs of a nearby landmass,
signs of our enemy.
Swords, axes and spears thrown
into the hearts of Europe,
bishops and priests.

        I watch, on guard
        as my brother paces the bar,
        bumping patrons and staining
        their fancy clothes.
        Their mingled colognes
        smell like a church gathering,
        and we are
        the devil's stink.

Using religion against them, we snickered
beneath our helmets, claiming
that our leader had died
and wanted a Christian burial to atone for his Viking sins
only to have him jump from the coffin of his own funeral
and stab the officiating bishop,
then kill in anger once the laughter had died
all men of the city.

        My brother shoulders a man
        and the man tries to stand
        solid as stone. My brother
        offers to shake the man's hand
        but draws back and clutches the man's throat
        instead, digging thumbs
        to the man's spine.

            I reach
            for my sword, my ax.

We turned them into bloody eagles
by tearing out their deflated lungs
and spreading them across their backs like wings,
wisps of red snow flying through the air—
Into our beards
went the hearts of Europe.

                    But this time, our
                    fists empty and outnumbered,
                    the alley swallows us
                    and a bum laughs
                    until our nostalgic shadows, riddled with blades,
                    swim across bricks.

I Ate Bukowski

I was Hungry for simple language
and ate Charles Bukowski.
Started with his bulbous nose
like a batch of grapes—
the juices of his oversized pores
shooting into my mouth
with each hungry chomp—
purple blood.

Then I took a rest,
kept from puking by remembering
just how bad the form poets had tasted.

The next morning I ate Bukowski's hands.
The skin there was sandpaper
from all the factory boxes and business envelopes
he had carried under thousands of lamp suns.
And the fingers—God—the fingers
were little sausage links
that tasted like rotting frog legs
except for the tips. They
tasted like the black enamel
of typewriter keys.

All that night
I spat letters of simple wisdom
about the blank walls
like *As the spirit wanes
the form appears*[1]
and nodded yes—
yessss.

---

1   from Art, by Charles Bukowski

The next day I was even more hungry
and ate his thick thighs in one sitting,
clamped them between my teeth
and reared back to tear the muscles.

This made me tough.
Turned me into every Bukowski imitator—
Bad Ass,
except it only lasted
one night.

I threw that fucker's feet out the window
and used his arms to club my couch.

This strenuous activity
really worked the appetite
so I decided I better eat his brain
before I turned into a dumb ass.

But
directly after I unhinged his skull
I had a revelation.
Cut his mind to bits
and snorted the thin pieces.

They wriggled inside my head
like strip teasing worms.

I became very anxious
and cracked a beer.
Then another
and another
until I shouted, "Jesus I am not going to eat
your stinking guts, *Bukowski!*"
and hoped that my own liver would do.
Chainsawed everything below his chest off

(balls, and purple onion cock included)
then glared at his nipples, cracked more beers
until I shouted, "Jesus I am not going to eat
your stinking nipples, *Bukowski*!"
and tore them off with my nails,
reunited them with his feet.

The holes in his chest looked dark and deep
as the tops of uncorked wine bottles
through which faint echoes
drifted out
as if from inside a cave.

Some thing
was still alive
inside that dead man. I reached
and pulled out his heart.
It fluttered and bulged
when a small beak poked through
and a bluebird's head popped out.

The little bird began to screech
frail as it was,
feathers so sparse from being trapped
in that dark bloody heart
that it spread its beak up at me as if I were its mother
while trying to waddle its weary body
through all of that red mush
so I did what was right
and certainly needed—

I cupped   the bluebird in my hands
and regurgitated   Charles very carefully,
very slowly   into its little mouth
but his knowledge   will forever dance
in my head   like strip teasing worms
waiting   for the next
hungry writer.

A Bumble Bee Sting, Pull It Out & Walk Away with Black & Yellow Striped Knowledge

Last night I dreamt of werewolves masturbating into the heads of bullfrogs.
When I awoke there were voices streaming from my fan,
little whispers—*pssst, pssst, pssst—pssst, pssst, pssst—*
Where are these words coming from?

Life Lesson:

If you put your phallus in the mouth of a woman
you are subjecting millions of babies to acidic hell.
If you put your phallus in the vagina of a woman
you are subjecting millions of babies to a more than Christ-like resurrection
where they are all to die but one who subsequently turns into a giant
baby killer who will feel the unexplainable urge for breasts or cocks
or asses or vaginas or mouths and maybe even feet. I hear in Alaska
they prefer to lick armpits. And where did we come from? Why
the coming of God, of course. All over the ovary Earth
like a greenish blue eyeball. And it stung.

Right now, wherever readers are in the future of these words
I am God—the creator of their current state of imagination.
I have erected a rather whorish shlong of language
and spit it all over the minds' eyes. Does it sting
to question all the bullshit taught before this?
What makes one think I don't get this from a higher power?
After all, I am living in a cum bubble full of retarded fish
swimming like Christopher Columbus to find niggers and injuns
to kill. Where did the KKK come from? And why
do they dress up as sperms?

It stung all right, it stung. And we are slowly being digested by God's humanity,
straight into the eyeball. Now everyone put lights on the tree
and gifts underneath. Don't forget the gay Hallmark cards—
we saw one of us born to be resurrected, and he is *more* than a giant baby killer.
Much more. He *is* the baby killer of the cosmos and his phallus *is* the milky way;

and when you see the sun, that is God's urethra pissing gamma rays;
and when you see the moon, that is the hole out of God's ass.

And I'm not just talking about the religion of whites, but all.
And I would smear those beliefs on poison ivy too, if only I knew them,
because they are aware as well as I, that we just don't know.
But why not strap a bomb to your chest
and give me a hug, anyway, for I assure you
I do, I do, I do
(saying on one knee)
believe in God.

A Stupid Smart Poem over the Trolley Microphone

Imagine not knowing any labels—
just seeing—*not knowing not knowing,*
but figuring like baby retinas.

I don't want to look at the sky and see
big or little dippers. I want
to see stars.

I don't want to look at a map and know
the name of a mountain. Just knowing
it is a mountain is quite too much already.

I don't want to see the northern lights and call
them that. Nor do I want words or meanings
for spirits or ghosts. I want to see the mystics
and want to want to leap.

Do not tell me I am a human,
or a man, and everything associated with.
Do not tell me I am an animal;
I have not the softness of the doe,
nor the sharpness of the alligator or
the push bomb buttons of the people.

I am a do not label my mother Amy,
but next I am a do not label Jesus Jesus
or God God, just let
us all am.

I am that in your words.

Do not see a corpse and call
it that, unless that is your own name for it.
Nor say death did that, or that
the dead smell bad.

How do you know what smells bad?
Everything just smells!
Some like the smell of their own shit
but the smell of others is ruined
when they are told so.

Everything can be good and unique
like the blind boy who ventured outside
and caught the scent of something sweet—
a perfume of course, or . . . *no,*
a rabbit that passed away—
its decompose wafting.

Nursing homes smell like
meatloaf.

Dog ass smells like
nirvana.
Ask them—they'll bark!

Huh

Donovan was a childhood friend,
the kid from grade school
who comes to your 7th birthday party
and eats McDonalds with you.

He had short brown hair cut with a bowl
and was funny lookin' with freckles.

I went to his house once and
only once.
His mother wouldn't let us play
with G-I Joes.
Deemed them immoral
and me immoral
for having plastic on plastic
slaughter fests.

She only let us play with firetrucks
and policemen with no guns,
whew whew whew whew.

But when Donovan grew up
he became a sniper in the Iraq war.

Killed
who knows what
how many times.

And when he came home
he took his own life
who knows how.

His grainy smile stares back at me now
inked within the newspaper,
still the goofy lookin' kid
I once knew
sort of.

By crinkling the paper
I can make the lower half of his face move
up and down so as to speak

"What's   the   mor-   al   now,   Ma?"

The Man Who Cut Me Since Twelve

Paper scotch taped to the door, black words in marker:
Dad won't be able to work Saturdays.
The smell of his diminishing, there is no name for
but it registered in my nostrils when I stepped inside the barbershop:
        old scent death.
He looked up with hollow eyes, dark rims, bruises—
        my barber?

"Hey there old timer," he jokingly croaked to me,
his twenty-four-year old customer, another young longing.
I didn't reply as fast as I'd have liked, was set back
for just three weeks ago this man was a bit overweight, healthy like,
but his skin had become short pale drapes over weak forearms
and when he turned to get the electric razor there were tendons of bony nape,
        two sticks of bamboo wrapped in human.

Aesthetic, I immediately felt a great sadness for this barber who had cut me
                since I was twelve.

    How, how, how'd *this* happen?
    How, how, how *so* fast?

        The diabetes? Cancer?

           No no:
           cirrhosis of the liver.

Instead of the usual "How you doing?" I asked "What's your daughter been up to?"
"Trouble," he said with a weak voice, "always trouble," turning with razor,
        slow asteroid thrown off course, budging
              through universe, pushing
                  through *air*
              as if it were infinite jelly.

    "What about you?" he asked.
    "Me? Awe—*trouble*," I said

and he tried to chuckle but coughed and tugged my head with scissors
then cleared his throat and asked, "Found a job?" "Looking," I said.
"How hard?" he asked. "Moderate," I said, and at this he didn't laugh
whether it was too difficult or because he was an old-school hard-worker,
I felt a little ashamed, though I was having problems of my own
     with auburn drink and autistic anxiety
     but nothing compared to six-foot grave
     headstones of carved last names:
          death.

"Taking your girlfriend out tonight?" he asked.
"No—no, she's out of town," I lied to cheer him,
     to make him think I was getting the most out of life,
          fucking
          young.

"Where's she live?" he asked. "Madison," I said.
     "Madison?" "Yea, Madison."
"Do you go down there to visit her, or does she come to you?"
     "She comes mostly," I said. "Must be desperate," he said
     and at this I had to laugh,
               verily archaic wishes.

From then on the whole haircut, like most things, was ruined
by my worried thoughts. I kept thinking he was going to slip
with the scissors, shaking so, and take one of my eyes out.
I slightly jerked when he came nearer with rusty blades,
          claws of crab.
I hoped he didn't notice. Tufts of old and new hair haloed our feet
with silver and brown and blonde glowing in morning floor sunlight.

For the finish, he grabbed the razor again, turning this time with the cord
          as if dancing with a listless ghost.
Then he unveiled my chest, carried the clippings gently to a basket.
No words came for the perfect goodbye. I simply said, "Thank you,"
and headed for the door, glanced back, "See yuh later," frog in throat.

"Stay out'ah trouble," he said, shaking youth out of comb, downcast eyes on falling hairs. "Yup," I said, fumbling and failing upbeat.

"Bye, bye," he said...

And that was it.
Done. Gone. It.

But what—
where is *it*?

Nobody knows.

So I went to Riverside park to think on it
where women beautifully jogged by the Mississippi,
and old fogies sat on benches contemplating *it*
    with me, old soul.
Seagulls called. Little girl—*little* little girl in a sage dress
handed me popcorn, said, "Here mister, feed da birds."
I smiled. Little girl! dancing tornado whirls in untied sneaker,
    throwing morsels. She fell, scraped a knee.
I chucked corn and the seagulls' eyes were dryer than ours.

All those tiny black eyes, what do they see?
    What do they know of death?

Old man, it may be nothing you're headed to,
    but so what if it is?

Nothing is perfect. Nothing *is* perfect!
    Perfection is...
                *nothing*ness!

It can't even be imagined it is so perfect.
    No art, nor color,
    nor life, nor death.

I hopped back in my car and looked in the visor mirror.
My bangs were crooked—too long, too short—
Thanks for nothin', old barber in eye of gull, going to sleep dreamless

per*fection*

Everything & Nothing

A hawk eats a blackbird in my backyard
for twenty minutes, holding it down with talons
while sucking guts, pausing for a moment
with a skinny leg and clawed foot
dangling from its maw
       then gulp,
sort of like a cannibal, sort of like a distant
       cousin,
the hawk picks the blackbird's life
       to pieces
and scans the land with jerky
       sharp eyes—
takes in the horror of the cardinals, the sparrows, the mourning
       doves—
then shits a long white string over the
       leftovers:
a few feathers, half a beak.
       No bones.

Sleeping with The

When hearing that your best friend has drowned
the struggle enters your imagination
like no other.
It isn't like hearing of a random drowning
on the ten o'clock news
thinking *that's too bad*
and dismissing it thirty seconds after. No,
you picture your friend kicking, swinging
fighting *water.*
You even try to hold your breath
until you gasp
looking for air bubbles. You
see catfish combing eyes, pulling lids shut.
You see your friend puffed and flaking
in the bottom of your coffee cup,
in coffee the same color as the muddy river
where they dump sewage;
your friend's arms and legs spread, clothes and hair billowing,
the body lightly bouncing every time your hand jerks.
You take a tentative sip
choke with the reality of it,
of this real imagination,
then retch your hot coffee into the fish tank
only to pause
with the steam rising off the water like some eerie mist
to see a shoe sticking out of multicolored rocks
before the suckerfish's black, yellow rimmed eyes
gaze into yours.

Horripilation

My words—seashells upon the page.
My voice—the faceless sea at your ear,
heard in your head, deep and blue,
full of the bottom's dark wonders
with sharp fangs and soft fins aglow,
unable to step onto your land, but
hold them in your mind for a moment,
maybe forever,
and let thought be lucent with fear,
sadness, hate, love, and all the terrible
beautiful wonders of this life,
your life, our life: the world below and above
always looking.

Enamel Eyes

In the nursing home
she is blind, deaf,
and paralyzed from the neck down.

I give her a drink
first.

Then it's my duty
to strip her, clean
her bones, the skin
that hangs like deflated tires.

I wipe her face
and with my touch
she shivers, moans.

I change her diaper
and dress her
in the same long, loose black dress
every goddamned bedridden day.

I brush her dentures
and gently hold her mouth open,
a tiny hole of black,
gums purple as jelly,
her head squirms.

"Say ah," I say
to her broken drums
and try to jostle the false teeth
in, try to make her mouth
bigger, but it's never enough.

Gray pictures of her dead
mother and father and sister
smile at us, even blow kisses.

I imagine what it's like
to be deaf and blind and eighty
six and unable to move,
all alone with some stranger's
fingers in your mouth.

How far gone is her mind?
Does she know where she is?
That all her family is dead?
Hell, is it?

"Ah," I say,
"ah, ah, ah."

The faces of her family
don't know. Maybe she
doesn't completely know.
Maybe her mind is
like the photographs, gray
taken fifty years ago
blowing kisses.

The dentures won't go in
today. I begin to sweat,
to shake.

"Ah," I say, "ah,"
and begin to weep.

My tears fall
into her mouth.

She stops squirming,
sticks her tongue out
and tastes the salt of sadness
that rolls along her dry buds.

For a moment, she grins
toothless, knowing
someone, perhaps a mother
a father a sister a cousin a
long lost niece still weeps
for her.

"Ah," I say, "ah,"
and catch the kisses they blew.

My Brother's Life

It was the morning after
the night I had thrown
a shot glass at a woman.
The morning after the night
I had threatened to stab.
The morning after the night
of kicked in, broken doors
that I visited my brother's
wife, the last remnants of
a Crown Royal bottle in my hand.
A therapist was there
playing with my Autistic nephew
quietly in the other room
as I stood in the corner of the kitchen
watching my brother's wife wash dishes,
drapes pushed aside the little window
above the sink, the sun coming through
with a bellyful of bird chirps and golden light
to illuminate her Mexican, African, Indian face.
Beautiful. I stood in awe and
for once my lips were parted, my nose not efficient
enough to let out the small gasps
that rose directly from my heart valves.
It wasn't just love. It was envy mixed with love
and happiness for my brother, as my nephew's laughter
slinked in from the other room
and I brought the bitter smooth whiskey
to my parted lips. This stupid beauty
I'll never be intelligent enough to understand,
for after all the mean, nonsense I've written,
for after all the violent, sad, lone nights
trying to obtain something great
I envy you this, brother, today.

Wise Asses in Love

My grandma's awake
in the psych ward
as I write this
tonight.

She's looking out
reinforced glass
for the moon
but it's on the
other side
of many
locked doors.

She's shuffling
her slippers
wishing for
shoelaces
to try and end it
all, or better yet
a glass picture frame
with grandpa inside
so she can
shatter it and be
reunited.

My grandma doesn't sleep
nights, she only dozes when
we come to visit,
slouching in weighted chairs
too heavy to throw,
long gray whiskers
seething from her chin,
and when she awakes
she covers her jello
with ranch dressing
to make us watch her

eat it—a sign
for us to leave.

I love my grandma
more now that they
think she's crazy
because people think
I'm crazy too
and it gives us
excuses not to visit,
but when we
are together
people often comment
how we both look
so tired,
to which we say
save the insomnia
for the
wise.

My grandma's awake
tonight and I am
awake tonight too.

Searchers

Foolish knowledge made me void.
It took away love, the past, and gave me
present space. I could stare at my hands for days
and only feel the pulse of my neck
spill into my brain.

I had planned on telling you this foolish knowledge.
Heartbreaking. To no longer care.
For it was the reason I started this poem
and it makes me want to chop my fingers off.

Just know that it is there, this
foolish knowledge, this
loss of love and feeling and past
is always there
in your mind, past the green and red colors,
the afterimages of light
when your contemplative eyes close.

Do not find it.
Search, but always be preoccupied
with sex or work or children
so that you'll never quite get there.

Telling you this makes me realize that I am not completely void
yet.

I love you all
searchers
of this void.

Keep looking into my well
and I will only send up black balloons
with white ribbons

I promise.

And when I stop
it's because I'm staring into these hands
filled with foolish knowledge, bleeding
and then closing
ten stubs over palms.

Somewhere over the Rainbow Bluebirds Fly

They gave me a prescription
for a tank's worth
of Prozac
and I drank my portions
each night,
little beknown that one of
Prozac's adverse effects
surprisingly
is that it can induce
suicide.

It tasted like a cold metal
mint bullet.

A week into the tank's worth
I dreamt that I was a horse
dripping a black oily substance,
on my side grinding my hooves
into a gravel road to stand
but to no avail
as a crowd of leering people
came forth with torches lighting
their moon-like faces
cratered with retarded grins
and reflecting in my wide
terrified eyes
consumed with fear that they
were coming to murder me,
and all I wanted to do
was kill myself.

When I awoke
the fear from the dream
stuck to me like webs still being spun
by a giant black widow's ass
and for the first time I truly

knew what it was
to want
to die.

So truly that I'd even say
verily. It wasn't just a
thought, it was bursting
through my brain
like a cold metal
mint bullet.

I rose from the bed
and went into the bathroom
shaking, sat on the toilet
still wet with drips of piss,
hugging myself, my fingers reaching
all the way around for the spine,
and knelt my head between my knees
unbeknownst the smell of shit.

This lasted for how long
one does not know,
but I later found myself
back in bed with sweat
and only when the theme song
from *The Wizard of Oz*
came muffled through my walls
did the black widows recede
with their ass webs full of fear
and I, calmly, sat up to spit out
the cold metal
mint bullet.

Not Crazy

I read the things that I've written
and think that I am crazy.

This is not so—

For when I go outside
I'm always careful not to
crush the ants. Did you know
they vote where to live?
But if I catch them taking down
a beetle, my heart sinks.
Still, I do not intervene
with violence. Sometimes
I move the beetle to
a safer place,
a leaf.

And if a mosquito
lands upon my body
I let him get his fill. Mosquitoes
must eat too. It's not their fault
that they are made to eat
our blood. Only
when they fly into my eyes,
ears, or nostrils
am I offended.

This is how it is
with all bugs—

I was once at a lady's house
watching her dance in the kitchen
when she stopped to retrieve a shoe
and squished a daddy-longlegs.
She questioned my disgust
and I told her, simply, that

she was no good. That one day
something would squash her
and if I were present
there would be no qualm about it.

My whole being told me
I needed her sex
and I told my whole being
I didn't.

This, is perhaps, why
I think of such things.
Of bugs. Their small lives,
like mine, to be lived
because we have no choice.
Shitty or not shitty
buzzes the fly,
and vomits.

I read the things that I've written
and think that I am crazy.

This is not so—

I am here to save,
knowing that one day
an invisible hand
will smash all our thin flesh
and leave our eyes oozing
into the ground.

We needn't contribute
to that fashion.
We needn't kiss
any malevolent sex.
We needn't give in
to our whole beings.

I am fine.
Some would say blessed—
this I'm not certain of. But crazy?
No. This is not so.

In the Cold of Wisconsin

Evening. The pigeons are frozen
to the electric wire and the trees are breaking.
How do little sparrows make it in
dead winter? There's a black stray dog
that won't budge for my car. Thirty degrees
below. Only when I get out to help does he slump off,
snowflakes in his eyes. He can see
through the crystals that I'm a human.
"Not like the rest," I call to him
but the wind screams, shatters
the words of my icy breath
and I choke on them.

The Fierce, Pink Light

That heart attack
wasn't meant to kill him,
it was meant to let him know
that I love him and
want him to stick around.

The Closest I Get

Whenever I stare into the sky
I lose my balance.

As a kid
swinging on a swing set
I leaned back and gazed into
that vast blue.
I felt like it was going to
catch me.

Now, standing here
in an open field of snow
it feels like I'm going
to be sucked up
to who knows where.

It's akin
to being a baby—
the wonder of the sky,
always
the wonder—
as the flakes rain down
and melt upon my eyes.

When My Nephew Laughs

He jiggles and falls, glowing
new teeth amongst his dark
African-Mexican-
Caucasian-Indian-
skin. He rolls until there isn't air
for sound, mute hysteria
like a drug happiness.
All I have to do is lurch
forward and pretend the tickle,
a simple bogus of imagination
that sends him reeling
all over again. I am reminded
where it was.
Where it is now
watching him crumple with merriment,
my eyes new and fresh like the world
to a puppy without the hatred
of knowledge to kill.

Battle Island

At Black Hawk Recreation Park
I crouch with my six-year-old nephew
and gaze into Bad Axe River
once tainted red with the blood of fleeing Indians
all whom surrendered only to be massacred—
women, children, warriors.

Mosquitoes buzz about our ears
and my nephew refuses to swat them,
for he says they must eat too.

Instead, he upturns his half-white
forearm, while three suck the red out.
I can almost hear the gunshots.
The boat's cannon fire. Screams—
Give your blood to this land.

What Kept Those Stacked Boxcars from Tipping Off

Sitting here babysitting my nephew
while he watches a movie and keeps saying
"What the hell?" I can't help but grin.
Don't even correct him. It's nice to hear
him talk, however seldom. He has Autism
you see. Couple years ago you wouldn't hear
from him. I like to think I had a hand in
getting him to speak up. Telling him the difference
between Yes and No, and which one to use more.

A moment ago I asked if he'd like to go
outside. Just then the train came rattling by, speeding,
shaking loudly on those rails. I was wondering
what kept those stacked boxcars from tipping off
when my nephew turned, scowling with little hands
cupped over his ears and firmly answered
"No! Uncle Matt. Stay inside now!"
"Sure," I said, patted him on the head,
winked.

I don't mind. I know what it is to stay inside,
grab a notebook, pencil, but before I begin
I think of the past five days spent
hunting for a job. The horror of it. Real
horror. All those superior faces in
charge, and me shyly trying to explain
why I haven't worked for a year
and half, while thinking they can smell
my lavish laziness. Next week it'll be the same thing
over until they give me a chance. A failure's
chance. Shit, I can't even read when I'm in the midst
of that slavery. Can't sleep or write but
I am pretty good at drinking until
it's all gone and I'm shaking
like virgin animosity.

136

Today is different though. Today is
beautiful! Sitting here with my quiet
nephew. Drinking iced tea, notebook
resting in lap. No visitors, phone calls.
Leisure! I spoke no more than twenty words
today, gave no fake grins. It's all
real. And last week I worried my ass off
about everything, words included. Always
words like women. Lovers. Calmly now I feel
they've returned, pick up a book, sniff
its pages. Knowledge, ah! I love you
bitch! And next week I won't be able to breathe
again, I'll walk around like a mad zombie
application in fist, hand it to the so-called boss
man, and finally be able to give him a big
corny ass fake grin. Remembering today. Today.
Saturday.

Demetrius Already Knows

My nephew Demetrius
never understood why
when he was a child
that we played with
his brother instead of him.

His brother who, in the beginning
wouldn't look anyone in the eyes
or speak, who would shake
like Eve's apple tree as if
he were dropping apples of death
before us, his mind terrified
by the notched texture of a
wood table, and when fall came
he wouldn't dare play in the leaves.

My nephew Demetrius never understood why
we had to play with his Autistic brother
instead of him, and to spite us
he began to read before he even knew how
to crush us with early wisdom.
The solitary act, the old adage
wisdom is bleak
and it certainly is when you're that young.

Now, older, we take Demetrius sledding
and it's his brother who's left out
simply because there are things he refuses to do.
But when we come upon a hill full of children
Demetrius refuses too. His father, sensing his son's
antisocial trepidation
says, *"People don't matter."*

Demetrius already thinks he knows.
Even writes poems about us now—
like me, his uncle, which he writes

138

that I smell like dead meat
for I smell so bad it made all
the soldiers dead from WWII.

Judging by the poems
I write about family
if that isn't a hint
of karma to come
I don't know what is.

My Brother Was Crazy

I didn't turn the light off
before bed
tonight.

Instead I lay here
in the soft yellow glow
thinking about my nephew
crying,
nine years old
with an Autistic brother.

My nephew was crying because
kids at school had picked on his brother
for being different.

I told him
it would pass
but it would seem
like a very long time
before it truly passed,
before people finally
grew up.

There will always be children
I told him,
but your brother
is going to make you exceptional
and he is going to remain
exceptional for you.

There have been geniuses
with Autism
I told him,
and regardless
you are both going to become
real men, wise

before the other kids
and you are both going to be
stronger men than the others
in the end.

I think about this all
tonight
under the soft yellow glow
of my lamp
while I should be sleeping
in the dark like the others
rising early to hunt and be
just so-called men

but at least I'm writing
and I know that the death
of a gunned down bird
is no victory.

That's what
the light is for.

Brothers

Drunk, I cracked
my brother's head open
on a rock.

When I ran
he was quick
to get up.

The only thing
that saved me
was when I was little
he had smashed my head
repeatedly
onto a couch's wooden armrest.

Either way,
we're brothers.

A Disgusting Poem about Love

My brother shared
an ice-cream cone
with his son.

They took turns
licking it.

This might sound okay
to some of you,
but my brother's tongue
was caked a bumpy rust
with hangover residue,
and his son
eats boogers.

Did I mention
the acidy hangover belches
spewing stink
from my brother's lips that hot day
strolling around Ann Arbor,
or that his son
only brushes his teeth
once a week?

I thought it was about love.
It had to be about love! I thought,
and then I asked my brother
before heaving into a cigarette disposal,
"At what point does one
find it okay to share
an ice-cream cone?"
having noticed in the past
how he and his wife
would wet the baby's pacifier
with their own saliva
before sticking it back in the baby's mouth,

thinking this was perhaps
how things came to the point of
a thirty-year-old
sharing a cone with
a seven-year-old,
or maybe it all started
with the first simple swipe
of poop
off a diaper smeared ass.

My brother turned to me,
caught off guard by his own actions.
"Well…I…uh," he stammered,
"don't friggin know."

And then his son looked up at me,
the sun squinting his eyes, the
ice-cream beginning to drip
onto his shirt again, his
little mouth too small to keep up
with the melting cone,
"Mom told him to help me."

"She did, eh?" I said. "Awe, that's sweet—

maybe someday
your mom will tell you about
daddy's gingivitis."

Payback

I can hear my father farting
in the next room.
Tomorrow he'll rise early
for work
and finally I'll be able
to sleep
and when I awake
there will be food for us both
provided by him.

I sure hope
he keeps on farting
because I write
when I can't sleep
and maybe someday
when he's too old
I'll be able
to take care of us both
and he can lay awake
listening
to me.

The Fierce, Pink Light

My father, in old age,
puts seeds upon his hat
to feed the birds
and I can't understand—
　　the mouse snapper
　　the deer hunter
　　the bat drowner
that he was.
But when a wheel
smudges a robin's wing
to the road,
it is my father, too,
that comes to save life
by unsticking the stunned bird
from the cars' path and placing it
in a shoebox,
then carrying it to the backyard
where he watches it for
hours, watches it until
it finally hops away
when the sun has turned
pink. My father
　　the mouse snapper
　　the deer hunter
　　the bat drowner
that he was—
this is the bravest
I ever saw him—
the fierce, pink light
washing death from his upturned face.

Still

I'll never grow up
I used to say to my mother
and balance as many heavy books
as possible on my head.
Holding her hand
and following her around the house
I did chimp talk
and itched my pits,
her little monkey.
I wish you'd never grow up
she used to say
and I said I won't
I won't
I won't
but damnit
tonight I'm half a foot
taller than her,
drinking a forty.
Oh Mathias, she says,
I wish you'd grow
your hair back.
But I keep shaving it
and shaving it to the scalp
with three razor blades,
then bending for her to feel
the scalp's smoothness.
Touch the dolphin I say,
all grown up.
It doesn't feel like a dolphin
you stupid son-of-a-
bitch she says,
and I laugh.
Despite this transformation
not too much has changed.

I Only Dance for My Mother

She gives me the wine
and I take the wine.

I mop her floors
and she walks on them
while they're still wet
so I begin to dance
to warn her of how
easy one can slide.

She watches
grinning in her old green jacket
before going outside
to see the moon on the snow.

A Premonition about Readings

(to be read out loud)

One thing about being a negative writer
and being paid to be a negative writer
is that you're expected to appear in public
and the people want you to be nice
in person, they don't want to shake the hands
of a chronic masturbator, they want a smile
not a frown, they don't want you to stammer
and just about piss yourself when you begin
to read, they want you to have a hard on
tucked under your belt and a tail to wag
and thrust up their skirts—but fuck, not butt fuck,
but fuck—I just can't put up with this shit.

All Eyes on Me

I arrived at the pharmacy
just before it closed,
twenty-six years old,
picking up my
blood pressure pills.

All the shaking
old people, remembering
just in time, stood in line
with me, the young man,
but all of us late.

Then I saw him—
a man between young and old
missing an eye.

His hollow socket was a void
but I swear something glimmered inside
the black cave of his skull.

He was buying vitamins

when he slightly turned
as if his eye were still there,
as if to gaze at me,
and I swear I had
always been the strange one
no matter what
but never before had I seen it
so clearly.

When God Thinks about Me

I see old poets
who have read my work
and then died
possibly going to God
and answering questions
about me.

Yes, he is a decent writer.

But what of does he write?

The dead old poets
scowl, curl fingers
over their upper lips,
think.

He writes of forsaking his father
and becoming a man
highly sensitive and in need of crutches.
He writes of women writers
that he jerks off to and
male authors he cannibalizes.
He writes of the breasts
of his brother's wife, how
the nipples look upon him like dark eyes
thinly veiled by a white t-shirt,
and how the moon holds
a retarded grin
while he stares at its glow in the black sky
imagining it is
the hole out of your ass.

God considers all of this,
runs a Godly tongue over Godly lips,
and smiles a Godly smile longer than the Milky Way.

Where I Go To Read

Hiawatha, the fifty foot Indian,
stands at Riverside park
next to a cannon pointed at the sky
under an American flag.

Why? I don't
want to know.

A big plastic reindeer body
stands without a head.

Why? Hia-
watha! *Why?*

A man in army pants
and a green parka squats
to pick from the icy snow
frozen bread crumbs
meant for ducks.

And the ducks laugh
while sliding across
the half frozen river.

This is where I go
to read.

Even in winter
I am pretending
to look for a job.

When I need to stretch my legs
I get out of the cold car
and walk the circumference
of the park, past all the dying
Christmas trees lying in the banks.

Going by old people in idle cars
the clicking of their door locks
make me scoff at how serious they are
about dying easy.

By the time I make it
all the way around the park
my head is so cold I am drunk
with the winter of life.

I stop beneath a tree
to watch a courageous squirrel
study my face,
only a foot away.

The squirrel
doesn't budge.

No-locks-nature
is my friend.

I get back in my car
and still hear the laughter
of the ducks.

As the car warms
my head
their laughter fades.

Only then
do I drive away,
waving.

Nightmare

---

*They happen
every night
and day.*

The Last Visit

It was dark in the living room
but for the TV's blue flickers—
my father was sitting in a recliner
in his underwear, remote in hand;
my mother was lying on the couch
arm over forehead, eyes closed;
my brother and I sat cross-legged
on the floor, when I got the urge
to peek at the thunderstorm and went
to the front door, parted the blinds.
Staggering like a corpse but still alive,
Grandma was out in the rain, coming
toward the door, disarrayed with bald-spots,
sparse curls smeared down one side
of her slack cheeks, mouth open,
rain dripping from her brow and nose—
soaked—sinewy hands
reaching for the knob.
Lightning. I let the blinds fall closed
and turned to my family. *Grand-
ma's here*, I croaked. My father's eyes
darted; my mother sat up from the couch
instantly woken; my brother made as if to crawl
but was numbed deaf and dumb with shock.
No, my father whispered. I couldn't speak.
We listened, the TV on mute, rain pattering,
all silent but for an occasional rumble
of distant thunder. *I swear it!* I squealed
and ran to the darkest corner to hide.
Then I saw from the new angle
the silhouette of my grandma's head
outside a different curtain-less window,
the passing headlights illuminating her
off and on like a strobe, but it was just her brow
and sparse curls in view, dyed red, gleaming
wet and long in the night as if reaching

for something, a few sticking to the glass.
She must have forgotten how to knock on the door
or ring the bell. *She's at the window*, I whispered,
voice shaking, barely audible. Everyone turned.
Their heads careened trying to make her out.
My father flicked the TV off and sat forward.
Completely dark now, inside and out, not even headlights.
The quietest *tap-tap-tap* came from the window.
We all glanced at each other but didn't move.
We knew she couldn't see us. Silence again.
No one breathed. A minute passed. Two minutes.
We began to relax, when an orange
crashed through the glass and put a juicy crater
in the wall above my head—Grand-
ma was home from the psych-ward.

Mathias Nelson lives in Wisconsin.